M·A·G·I·C
Made Easy

NEWLY REVISED EDITION

M•A•G•I•C
Made Easy
by Larry Kettelkamp

DRAWINGS BY LORING EUTEMEY
photographs by Donovan Klotzbeacher

William Morrow and Company
New York   1981

Library of Congress Cataloging in Publication Data

Kettelkamp, Larry.
  Magic made easy.
Includes index.
1. Tricks—Juvenile literature. 2. Conjuring—Juvenile literature.
I. Eutemey, Loring. II. Title.
GV1548.K4   1981   793.8   80-22947
ISBN 0-688-00458-X
ISBN 0-688-00377-X (lib. bdg.)

Contents

Introduction

*

The magic tricks in this book are easy enough so that any boy or girl can learn to do them. All of them can be set up with ordinary household items. Some of the tricks will almost work themselves; others will need practice. A few have several parts to remember. And many can be grouped together to make interesting combinations.

To become a good magician, you will want to follow some helpful hints:

1. *Have Your Materials Ready*

    Read the directions carefully to find exactly what you need to make or use. Take time to prepare it properly. Double check to make certain everything is on hand.

2. *Memorize Your Story and Motions*

    For most tricks there are two very different things to learn: the mechanical steps you do to make them work and the story you tell for the audience. Go through the motions until they are automatic. Then memorize the story until you can tell it without making a mistake. Stories are suggested for many of the tricks. Or you can make up your own. But in either case both the story and the actions must be memorized.

3. *Practice in Front of a Mirror*

   A trick is only as good as it appears to the audience. Practicing your story and motions in front of a large mirror will show you exactly what the audience sees and does not see.

4. *Test Each Trick on a Friend*

   After you have memorized the story and motions and viewed everything in a mirror, you still need one more aid. Do the trick for a close friend or family member who will be honest with you. If your friend likes the trick, it is probably ready for performance. If not, practice again until you can do it smoothly and correctly.

5. *Be a Real Actor*

   To be a good magician, you must become a real actor. Speak slowly, loudly, and clearly. Look at your audience. Act excited. And try to imagine that real magic is taking place. Once you are convinced yourself, your audience will also become convinced.

Part I
MAGICAL ILLUSIONS

Magic is possible because things around us are not always what they seem to be at first glance. The tricks in this chapter all take advantage of this fact. Some are optical illusions. Others are illusions of balance or motion. Although the tricks are easy starters, all of them are both amusing and surprising. When set up properly, these illusions will almost work themselves.

✳ X-RAY TELESCOPE

This first trick is an optical illusion. Using a special viewing tube, you can make your hand look as if there is a big hole right in the middle of it. The only gimmick you need is a hollow tube about five inches long and a little more than an inch wide. An empty bathroom-tissue roll will work perfectly. Or you can make a tube from heavy paper five inches long and four inches wide. Roll it up from the five-inch edge, overlap the edges slightly, and tape or glue it together.

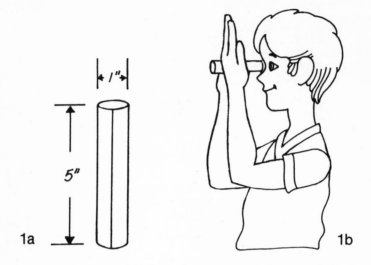

1a

1b

Hold the hollow tube to the eye you would use for looking through a telescope. Bring your other hand up beside the tube with the palm facing you. The hand should be a short distance from the far end of the tube. With *both* eyes open, look at some object ten or fifteen feet away. As soon as you focus on the distant object, you will notice an enormous hole in the middle of your hand. At the same time, you will seem to be viewing the distant object clearly right through that hole!

The secret is to look at the distant object as you normally would with both eyes open. One eye sees the object through the tube. The other eye sees the palm of your hand. Your brain combines the two views to make

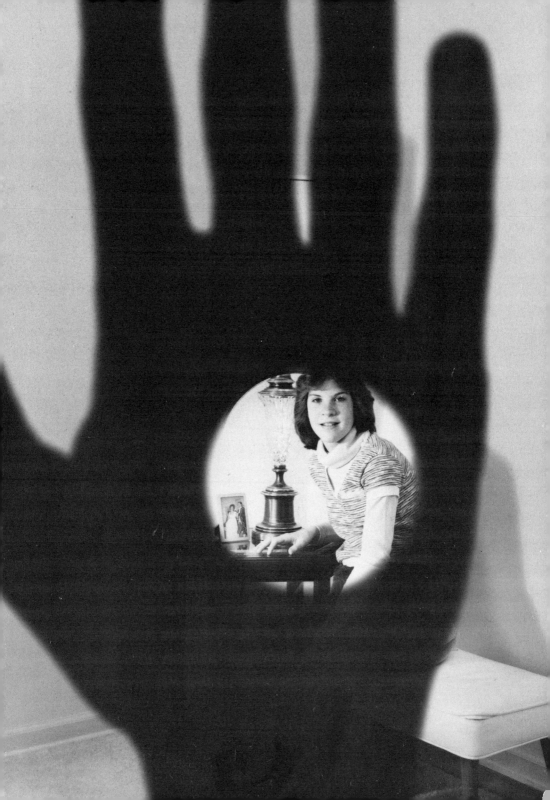

the X-ray illusion. You can jokingly tell your friends that you have developed a magic telescope that contains a new kind of invisible X-ray gas. The result is startling even when you know it is an illusion.

✳ RUBBER PENCIL

Here is a trick in which a pencil looks as if it is made of rubber. Use a long pencil. Pinch the eraser end between thumb and first finger as shown in figure 2. Now hold the pencil sideways as you shake your hand gently up and down. If you hold the pencil somewhat loosely, the pointed end of the pencil will start to move up and down a little while the middle of the pencil stays in

2

about the same place. The pencil moves like a seesaw. When your hand jiggles quickly enough, the images of the moving ends blur, and the pencil looks as if it is flopping and bending like a piece of soft rubber.

Explain to your friends that you have bought a pencil for people who make too many mistakes. The whole pencil is made of rubber so that it can be used as an eraser. Then shake the pencil so it seems to wobble and flop. Your friends will want to try the trick themselves.

✳ SOLID THROUGH SOLID

In this illusion a solid wooden matchstick seems to pass through a solid safety pin. To prepare the trick, you need a wooden match and a very large safety pin. With a pair of scissors, cut off the head of the match. You may need to rotate the match gradually as you do so. The two ends of the matchstick should look the same. To find the middle of the stick, cut a strip of paper just as long as the stick. Fold the paper in half, and use it to measure *exactly* to the midpoint of the matchstick. Mark the point with a pencil dot.

Now open the large safety pin. With a pair of pliers, grip the middle of the match and carefully insert the point of the safety pin into the match at the pencil dot.

Twist the pin around and around to work a hole through the match gradually. Go slowly. The wood *must not split*. If it does, start again with a new match. Once the hole goes all the way through, you can push the pin through again from the other side. Close the safety pin. Wiggle the match around until it is loose enough to turn very easily on the pin.

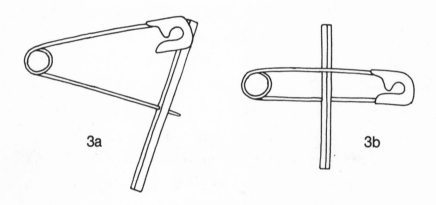

3a

3b

Now you are ready for the trick. Hold the safety pin by the head as shown in figure 3c. Position it so that the match pivots on the lower bar of the pin. Rotate the match so that it touches the upper bar of the safety pin. Then pivot it back toward yourself just a little. Now with thumb and first finger, smartly snap the upper end of the match away from yourself. If the match is loose enough, it will hit the upper bar

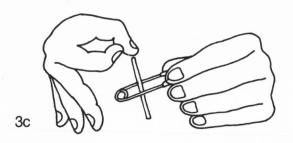

3c

of the pin and bounce back almost all the way around to the other side. The movement is so fast that the upper end of the match seems to pass through the upper bar. Actually the opposite end of the match has bounced back to appear on the other side. Because the pivot hole is in the middle of the match, the two ends look about the same.

At first, the match may not be loose enough on the pin to create the effect. But soon a gentle snap is all you will need to do the trick. Don't snap too hard, for then the matchstick may bounce twice and not end up in the right position. If you don't get the hole straight the first time, try another match. Remember that the wood must not split, because then the match will not be able to move freely on the pin. With a little practice, you will have a match and pin set that will work for a long time.

You can make up a story about mind over matter

or about the matchstick passing through a space warp to get to the other side of the safety pin. The trick is such a good illusion that even when the secret is known, the effect is still amazing.

✻ FLOATING SAUSAGE

This optical illusion is very effective. If you do it right, it looks as if a sausage is floating in midair between your fingertips. Hold your two first fingers about four inches in front of your eyes as shown in figure 4. Extend them so that the fingertips touch each other and the fingers form a straight horizontal line. The fingernails should be at the back, away from you. Keeping your fingers in place, focus on an object a little distance away. Even though you are not looking directly at your fingers and they are slightly out of focus, you can still see their shapes. You will also notice an extra shape like a sausage that seems to be stuck between the tips of your fingers. Pull the tips of your fingers apart very slightly, and the sausage will appear to float in the air between your fingertips.

4

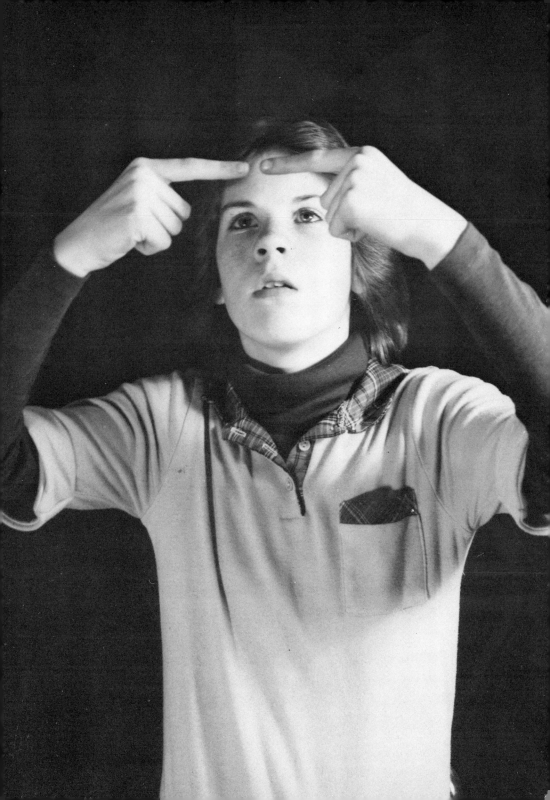

The illusion will only occur if you are focusing both eyes on a distant spot rather than on your fingertips. If you close one eye at a time, you can then discover how the images of your fingers actually overlap from left to right to produce the illusion of the sausage. This trick should get a good laugh from your friends who have not tried it before. The funny sausage looks very real indeed.

✳ MULTIPLYING MONEY

To change twenty-five cents into seventy-five cents magically, you need a quarter and a clear drinking glass. Put the quarter in the middle of the bottom of the glass. Make certain it stays in that position. Next pour about an inch of water into the glass, covering the quarter. Look at the glass from the side and slightly above the level of the water. When the angle is correct, you will see the quarter appearing to float on the water. And beneath the quarter on the bottom of the glass is a larger coin that looks like a fifty-cent piece. Your money has multiplied!

The curve of the glass acts like a magnifying lens to enlarge the quarter to the size of a fifty-cent piece at the bottom of the glass. At the same time, light rays reflected upward from the quarter bend toward your

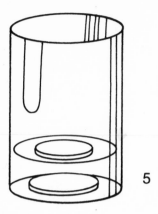

5

eyes as they leave the surface of the water, making the quarter appear to float on top. Ordinary light can play mysterious tricks to make you see double.

✳ ANTIGRAVITY CLAMP

This trick depends on a simple device cut from corrugated cardboard. A belt is placed in the slot at the top of the cardboard. Amazingly, the belt does not fall even when the device is supported at only one end.

First you will need to trace the pattern shown in figure 6a. Put a sheet of carbon paper between the tracing and a piece of heavy corrugated cardboard from an empty carton. Cutting later will be easier if you place the pattern along one edge of the cardboard. Trace the same pattern a second time on another sec-

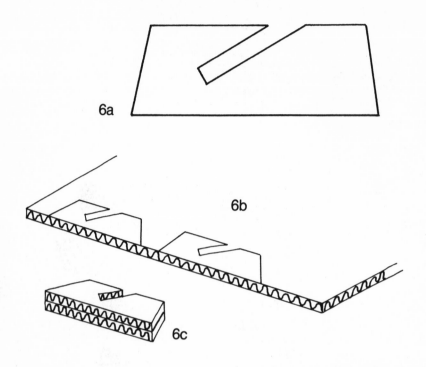

6a

6b

6c

tion of the corrugated cardboard. With scissors, cut out the two matching shapes. Cut along each edge of the slanting slots. Fold the slot tabs out to one side, and snip them off at the base of the slot. Glue the two corrugated cardboard shapes, flat sides together, with any white glue, such as Elmer's, as shown in figure 6c. Allow the glue to dry. You now have a sturdy, extra-thick "antigravity" clamp.

Find a fairly stiff leather belt; insert it in the slot of the clamp as shown in the photograph. The buckle

end will have to be shorter than the other end before the belt will balance. Make adjustments by sliding the belt back and forth in the slot. Once the belt is correctly positioned, you can put one corner of the clamp on your fingertip and the belt and clamp will seem to hang in midair with no support. Because of the angled slot, the belt is twisted so that the lower portions are actually beyond the supported end of the clamp. The belt and clamp are really in balance, even though they don't seem to be. The point of the clamp can also be balanced on the end of a pencil or the projecting corner of a table. The antigravity illusion is still the same.

To impress your friends, you can say that you have been given a special antigravity clamp that was found in an alien spaceship. It is used to turn ordinary belts into antigravity belts. Nobody will believe you, but the trick will work itself anyway.

✳ MYSTICAL MATCHES

For this trick, you need four wooden matches, a spoon, and a glass of water. Bend each match in the middle so that it cracks but does not break completely. There must be a thin strip of wood still connecting the two halves of the match. Bend each match into a square corner, and arrange the matches to form a

28

cross as shown in figure 7a. Use a smooth, waterproof surface such as a Formica countertop.

Dip half a spoonful of water from the glass. Carefully tip the spoon so that a large drop of water falls on the countertop just inside the square corner of each match. Do not let the spoon touch the matches.

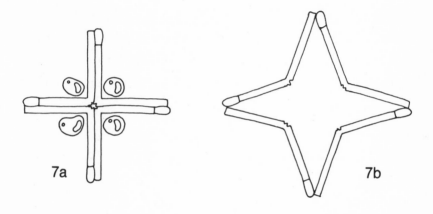

7a

7b

Each water drop will spread to touch the bent corner of a match. As soon as the wood becomes wet, it will expand, and each match will slowly try to straighten out. The center of the figure will open up, and within a few minutes the cross will have changed into a four-pointed star. In case any coloring from the matchtips stains the countertop, it can be removed later with powdered cleanser.

Here is the story you can tell as you follow the steps of the trick: "Ancient sorcerers believed that there were four mystical elements—earth, fire, air, and water. These four matches are made of wood that grows in the *earth*, and they also create *fire*. The third element, *air*, is all around us, and the last element, *water*, is in this glass. When these four mystical elements come together, true magic can take place. I am going to break these matches and arrange them into a perfect cross. Each arm stands for one of the four elements. By adding water the cross will be magically changed into a star. Four drops of water give us the mystical number we need. Will the power begin to work? Watch carefully. Yes, the magic is complete. The cross has become a star!"

Part II
HAND MAGIC

The tricks in this chapter all involve motions or skills with arms, hands, and fingers. They are what magicians call "sleight of hand." Some of these tricks use nothing more than the parts of your own body. Others require a few basic props, or gimmicks, that are easy to make. Even the tricks that look very difficult are actually simple to do. But you will want to practice them carefully in front of a mirror until the moves become automatic.

★ JUMPING RUBBER BAND

The effect of this trick is that a rubber band around your first two fingers jumps magically to the last two fingers of the same hand. All you need to do the trick is a thick rubber band about an inch and a half long.

First hold your right hand upright with the palm facing you. Put the rubber band around your first two fingers, and slide it down to the base of the fingers as

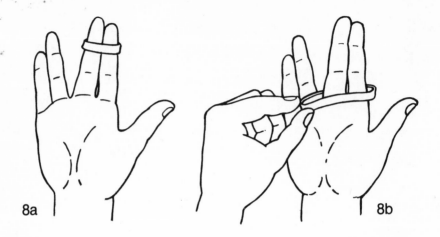

8a 8b

far as it will go. Pinch the rubber band between the thumb and first finger of your left hand. Stretch the band to the left across your palm as shown in figure 8b. Curl your right-hand fingers, and slide the tips into the long loop you have made.

The rubber band must cross your fingers at the first joint near the base of your fingernails, as in figure 8c.

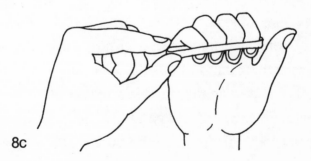

8c

Keeping your hand in a fist, turn it over so the knuckles are up. In this position, the rubber band appears to be wrapped around your first two fingers only. Now you are prepared for the magic. Quickly straighten out all your fingers. Amazingly, the rubber band will automatically jump to the other two fingers.

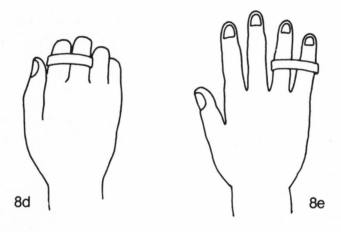

8d

8e

Naturally people must not know how the rubber band is fixed in advance. With practice, you can quickly set it in place before you announce the trick. You can use a story something like this one: "Most people have seen the small balls made of super rubber that have extra bouncing power. Here is a special rubber band made of this same rare super rubber. It has been found that heat has a strange effect on this kind of rubber. If someone will volunteer to help, I can show you how. I'm going to ask the volunteer to blow on the rubber band. The natural heat from the breath will act on the super rubber. Just blow gently on the rubber band, please. Ooops—there it jumps!"

✱ BROKEN ELBOW

Some surprising magic can be done using only your own arms, hands, and fingers. By combining this trick with the next one, you can present a silly story that looks more impossible with every step. The magician begins by saying that he was in an accident and that one arm has been very strange ever since. He extends his left upper arm straight out from the shoulder. The elbow is bent at a right angle letting the forearm and wrist hang down.

With the back of his right hand he flicks the left hand so the forearm swings back and forth loosely like a pendulum. He gives a stronger push, and the left forearm spins around in a complete circle like a propeller. The elbow joint seems to be completely disconnected!

The secret is to practice some special movements in front of a mirror. First hold the left arm out at a

9a

right angle as in figure 9a. Swing the forearm back and forth, toward the body and away again, so that it looks like a clock pendulum. Hold the upper arm very still so that *the elbow does not move*. The mirror will show you when the motion begins to look natural.

Now move the left hand out and all the way around in a complete circle. As the forearm comes straight up, *turn your left hand toward yourself* so that the elbow bends the usual way. This movement is the secret. If you move your forearm smoothly, no one will notice the slight turn of the hand. Be sure to hold the upper arm still. Follow this procedure in the mirror

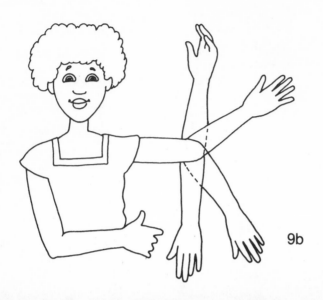

9b

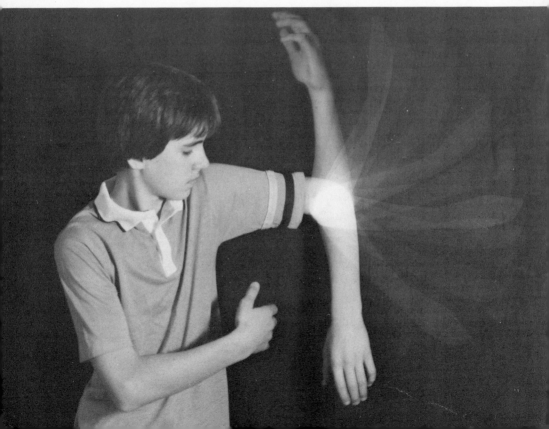

until your forearm rotates around the elbow like a perfect propeller. Now use the back of your right hand to start the left hand swinging. You can do two pendulum swings for each right-hand push. Then give a larger push for the complete propeller circle. When the spin is fast and natural, the effect is strange indeed.

✳ FUNNY FINGERS

The magician explains that ever since his left arm was in an accident, the fingers act strangely. First he shows that the left first finger has stretched. It is now much longer than the other fingers. Then he shows that another finger comes loose completely and wiggles back and forth at both ends. Finally he amazes the audience by pulling his left thumb off and setting it back in place. He then gives his left arm a shake to see if everything is all right again.

To make the left first finger look longer, the right first finger is added to it. First cover the *right first finger* from the base to the knuckle with the *left first finger* from the knuckle to the fingernail. Line up the fingers in the same direction. Now cross the right *middle finger* over the double first fingers. The extra fingernail will now be hidden. There apparently is only one much longer first finger. Use the mirror to see that

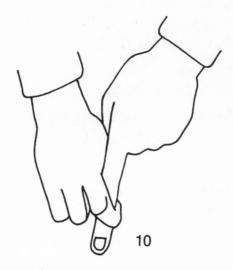

10

the fingers line up properly and the view is right for the audience. You can move the joined fingers up and down a little for effect.

To make the wiggly finger, there are three simple steps. First place the flat palms of your hands together. Bend the two *middle fingers* down so that the *left middle finger* is nearest you as in figure 11a. Keeping *all other fingers straight*, rotate your palms into the position in figure 11b. The fingertips of your right hand will rotate toward you as the fingertips of your left hand rotate away from you. *Only the middle fingers are interlocked.* Now there seems to be one loose finger poking up and down between your hands. Wiggle both middle

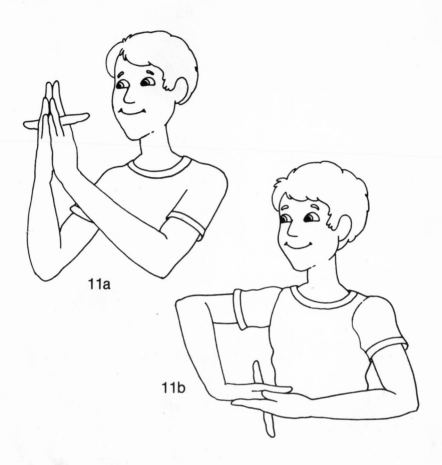

11a

11b

fingers at the same time, and the loose finger seems to have a life of its own. Remember that only the middle fingers should interlock as you follow the three steps. Use a mirror to check the effect.

To pull off your left thumb, you must make the tip of the right thumb look as if it belongs to the left thumb. First stand in front of the mirror. Hold your left hand facing yourself as in figure 12a. Bend the tip of the left thumb down so it does not show in the mirror. Hold your right hand with fingers pointing up.

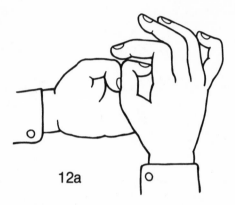

12a

Bring your right thumb from the base to the knuckle against your left thumb from the thumbnail to the knuckle. Bend down the tip of the right thumb. In the mirror, the right thumb tip will line up so that it looks like part of the left thumb.

Now with right first fingertip cover the gap between the two thumb sections. The mirror image should show what looks like an ordinary thumb, covered in the middle by the right fingertip. To create this natural effect, each thumb must remain sharply bent. Now you can slowly slide the right thumb tip back and forth along the left first finger. You apparently have pulled

12b

your thumb apart and then put it back in place! Keep your extra right fingers up, out of the way, so the action is clear. The mirror will show exactly what the audience sees.

To combine the funny fingers, loose thumb, and broken elbow into a single routine, you can tell a story like this: "Last week my left arm was almost broken in an accident. It has been very strange ever since. First I found that my elbow was loose and my arm would spin out of joint. Then I was surprised to find that one finger stretches longer than the others. And another finger comes loose and wiggles around. Sometimes even my

43

thumb comes right off, and I have to push it back into place. There, let me give the arm a shake to see if everything is together again."

✳ CRAZY COMPASS

The crazy compass works almost by itself, and it is not a hard trick to do. However, you must first make your own compass. With tracing paper or onionskin, trace the eight-pointed compass face and arrow outline shown in figure 13a. Using carbon paper, a sharp pencil, and a ruler, carefully retrace the design onto fairly

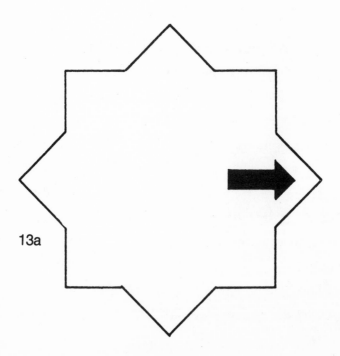

13a

heavy cardboard. You should not be able to see through the cardboard. Redraw the arrow outline with a black fine-line pen and ruler. Fill in the arrow with black ink. Very neatly cut out the eight-pointed figure exactly on the penciled lines.

Now hold the compass at opposite points between thumb and first finger as shown in figure 13b. The arrow must point away from you, at your first finger. Using as pivots the points you are holding, flip the compass over with the other hand. On the reverse side, you need a second arrow pointing to your right. Mark the location lightly in pencil. Use your original tracing and carbon paper to transfer a duplicate arrow to the back of the dial at the pencil mark. Redraw the outline of the second arrow with a black fine-line pen and ruler. This second arrow must exactly match the first arrow in size and shape. Fill in the arrow with black ink.

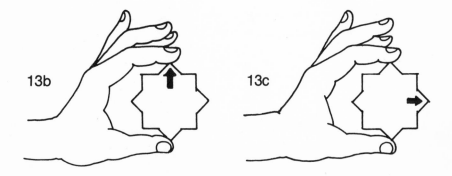

13b   13c

You are now ready to learn the moves and the story. Hold the compass again between thumb and first finger so the arrow points at your first finger. Begin by saying, "This is one of the craziest compasses I have ever seen. One time I used it on a camping trip. I was trying to go straight north, but I wound up going east." As you speak, flip the compass over, and the arrow will point to the east.

Now set the arrow at the angle shown in figure 13d, halfway between the north and the east positions as you continue your story. "The next day I tried the compass again. I wanted to go northeast, and the compass worked perfectly." At this point, flip the compass, and the arrow will still point in the same direction.

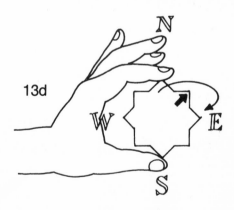

Now set the arrow pointing to the left, halfway between north and west, and go on with the story. "I decided the compass must be OK, so the next day I started off to the northwest. But I got turned around and wound up back where I started." As you finish speaking, flip the compass over once more. This time the arrow will point in exactly the opposite direction.

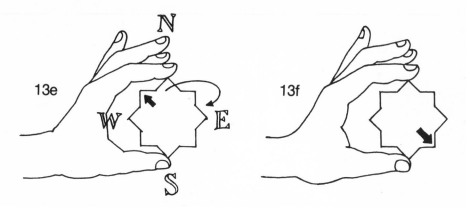

The three compass positions are easy to remember. First set the arrow to the north, pointing at your first finger. Next shift it one point to the right for northeast. Then set it one point left of north for northwest. Each time you flip the compass over it automatically comes up in the right position for the story. Everyone will agree that it is certainly a crazy compass.

✳ SILLY STRAW

This trick is a quick one that you can do between several longer ones. A short piece of soda straw appears to

be pushed into one ear and then to come out the other. To set up the trick, you will need a soda straw with no markings on it. A white straw that is fairly wide will show up best. Cut off a section a little less than three inches long. It should be a bit shorter than the distance across the palm of your hand.

Hold the straw at one end between your thumb and fingertips as shown in figure 14a. The straw should point in the same direction as your fingers. Now stand in front of a mirror. Hold the straw horizontally, with the back of your hand toward the mirror. Touch the

14a

end of the straw to your head just in front of your ear
as in the first photograph. Push your hand directly toward your head, sliding the straw between your thumb
and fingers. In the mirror, you will seem to have pushed
the straw straight into your ear.

Next move your hand to the other side of your head,

keeping the back of your hand toward the mirror. Rotate the straw with your thumb and forefinger so that it lies across your palm and curl your fingers around it. Turn your hand upright as in figure 14c.

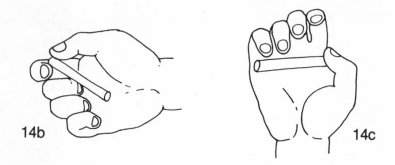

14b   14c

With the tip of your thumb, push on the end of the straw and it will slide straight out at the other side of your hand. You will need practice to get the straw to shift into the right position every time. And as you move your hand from one side of your head to the other, you have time to get your thumb tip on the end of the straw inside your fist. In the mirror, you appear to have pushed the straw straight into one ear, through your head, and out on the other side!

A good joke is to pretend that you are having trouble hearing. You can say, "Just a moment, my ears seem to be all stuffed up. Just let me run this soda straw through to clear them out. Oh, that feels much better." Do the steps of the trick right along with the joke. Then continue with another trick before anyone has a chance to wonder what really happened.

✳ ELEVATING ARM

This trick must be tried to be believed. Tell a friend that you can create a powerful force that will invisibly raise his arm. Ask your friend to stand with one shoulder leaning against a wall. Tell him to push hard against the wall with the back of his wrist and

15a

to keep pushing while he slowly counts to twenty-five. Then ask him to step away from the wall and relax. Within a short time, he will be astonished to find that his arm is floating up and away from his body as if something were pulling on it!

The secret lies in the muscles. All the time your friend is pushing against the wall, the shoulder muscles that would normally raise his arm out to the side are tensing. Later, after the arm is free, the muscles automatically respond again in a delayed reaction. But to

15b

the person doing the stunt, his arm feels as if it is moving about with a magical life of its own.

✳ MIND-CONTROL PROPELLER

The gimmick for this trick is a wooden stick with a cardboard propeller at one end. The stick has a row of notches along one edge. When you rub these notches with a pencil, the propeller will start to spin. Whenever you want to, you can make the propeller stop and spin in the opposite direction.

To make the magic propeller, you need a square stick of wood nine inches long, about three-eighths of an inch wide, and three-eighths of an inch thick. You can get sticks of wood such as pine, spruce, or basswood at a lumberyard or craft shop. You also need a piece of thin cardboard, a thumbtack, a straight pin with a large head, a smooth, round pencil or pen, and a ruler.

On the nine-inch stick make a pencil mark two inches from one end and another mark three inches from the other end. Mark off each quarter-inch along the edge of the stick, between the pencil marks. With a large, flat file or rasp, file a shallow notch into the stick at each quarter-inch mark. The notches should cut across the edge of the stick, as in figure 16a.

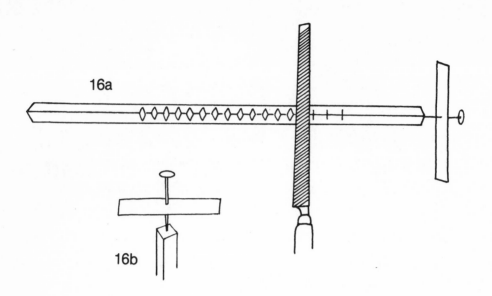

16a

16b

Next cut out a cardboard propeller three and one-half inches long and three-eighths of an inch wide. Use the ruler to measure one and three-quarters of an inch from one end, and put a pencil dot in the middle of the propeller. With the thumbtack, make a hole in the propeller exactly at the pencil dot. Also push the tack through the hole once from the other side. Then use the thumbtack to make a hole part way into the end of the stick nearest the notches. Remove the thumbtack. Push the large-headed pin through the hole in the propeller and into the hole in the end of the stick. Use pliers to insert the pin a little further into the stick, so that it fits snugly, as shown in figure 16b. Be sure the wood does not split. Adjust the pin so that it projects straight out from the end of the stick.

The propeller should now wobble around loosely on the pin at the end of the stick. If it doesn't, loosen it up a bit so that the slightest touch will start it rotating. If the hole is in the middle of the cardboard, the propeller will almost balance in a crosswise position. If it is out of balance, use scissors to trim a little off the heavy end.

The secret of controlling the propeller spin is to hold the smooth, round pencil (or pen) with your right hand, as in figure 16c. Your thumb is at the back and your forefinger is extended across the pencil. With

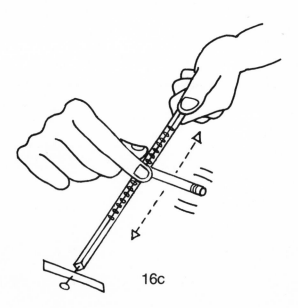

16c

your left hand, hold the stick firmly at the free end. Set the pencil across the notches, holding your right thumb on one side and the tip of your forefinger on the other side. As you rub the pencil back and forth along the notches, you will hear a vibrating sound. You can easily let either the tip of your thumb or the tip of your forefinger touch the wood of the stick as you slide the pencil along the notches. If *only your thumb tip* touches the wood just to the right of the notches, the propeller will start to spin to the left, or counterclockwise. If *only the tip of your forefinger* touches the wood just to the left of the notches, the propeller will start to spin to the right, or clockwise. Touch only the upper surfaces of the stick. Be sure that thumb tip and fingertip do not touch the stick at the same time, or the propeller will not turn. There must be only *one contact surface at a time*. Keep *either* your thumb tip or fingertip in *firm contact*, and the propeller will respond. No one will notice the slight shift in the position of your right hand. The sight of the propeller stopping its spin and reversing direction is truly startling.

Here is a story you can tell to go with the mechanical motions: "As you can see, this little propeller starts to spin because it is very sensitive to the vibrations

made by this pencil rubbing along the stick. It is also sensitive to the vibrations from my mind." As you begin to rub the notches with the round pencil, let only your right fingertip make firm contact with the stick. The propeller will spin clockwise.

Let your fingertip shift away from the stick and bring your thumb tip into firm contact along the other surface as you continue your story. "For example, if I concentrate hard enough, I can make the propeller stop and begin to spin the other way." By the time you get the words out, the propeller will have changed its direction. Now you can ask one of your friends to call out, "Change!" And by switching pressure back to only your fingertip, the propeller will respond by reversing again in a few seconds.

If your friends try rubbing the notched stick, the propeller is likely not to turn at all, or it will spin by accident, but only in one direction. They will have no idea how to control it to make it start, stop, and change direction on command unless you decide to share the secret with them.

Part III
AUDIENCE ROUTINES

The tricks in this chapter will work well in front of a group of people. The props and actions can all be seen easily from a distance. These tricks are not necessarily harder to do, but there are more steps to learn and you will need more preparation and practice. When you have mastered the tricks, you will be able to set up entertaining routines for a magic show in front of an audience.

✳ WANDERING WAND

A trick with a wand is always a good way to start a program of magic. You can make your own magic wand that will vanish and then reappear. To do so, you need several sheets of white typing paper, some black poster paint or India ink, and two wooden sticks about one-quarter of an inch wide. They can be either round wooden dowel rods or Tinker Toy sticks. One should be exactly eleven inches long, and the other should be about two inches long.

First lay the eleven-inch stick along the long edge of a sheet of typing paper. Put several dabs of glue along the stick. Roll the paper tightly around the stick, and glue the edge securely. Roll another sheet of typing paper tightly around the two-inch stick, and glue the edge of the paper securely. After the glue is dry, use a narrow object to push the short stick down to one end of the tube. You now have two identical-looking paper tubes. One has a solid wooden center. The other is hollow except at one end.

With a ruler, make a mark two and one-half inches from each end of each tube. With the black poster paint or India ink, darken the middle section of each tube between the markings. You now have two matching magician's wands, black in the center with white tips.

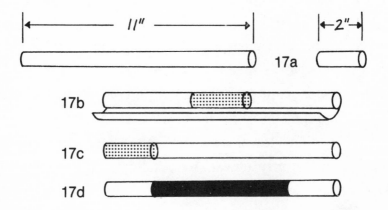

This trick makes a good opener for a magic program. In advance, place a sheet of newspaper on a table, and conceal the solid wand inside your shirt. When your audience is ready, walk quickly into the room, holding up the hollow wand between your hands.

17e

Here is how you can combine the motions and the story:

"Ladies and gentlemen, the first thing every magician needs is a sturdy magic wand." Rap the wooden end of the wand on the tabletop several times to demonstrate how solid it is. "I can easily hide the wand by wrapping it up in this sheet of newspaper." And as you speak, wrap the wand in the paper. "But of course, if it is a real magic wand, it ought to disappear completely."

Suddenly bend the newspaper roll in the middle and tear it into several pieces. The paper of the hollow wand inside will tear right along with the newspaper and will not be noticed. Drop the torn newspaper sec-

17f

17g

tions on the table, and rub your hands together as if you have completed a job well-done.

Reach inside your shirt for the duplicate wand as you finish your story. "But a good magic wand never loses its powers. Sometimes it turns up again where you least expect it!" Pull out the wand, and rap it on the table several times. To the audience, a perfectly solid wand seems to have vanished and mysteriously reappeared. While they are puzzling over the wand, you can move ahead to the next trick.

✳ PENETRATING KNOT

You can use the solid wand you have made for the next trick also. All you need is the wand and a good-sized handkerchief. You can use one of your own or borrow one from someone in the audience. Ask a volunteer to come up and help you with the trick. Shake hands, and ask the volunteer to hold one end of the wand with his left hand while you wrap the handkerchief around it. Position the volunteer to your left and stand sideways so that everyone can see what is happening.

Hold the handkerchief by diagonal corners and flip the loose ends around into a tight roll. Wrap the middle of the handkerchief roll around the center of the

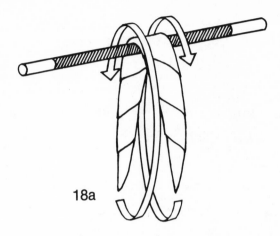

18a

wand as shown in figure 18a. Make sure each end
of the roll makes *one complete turn*. Ask the volunteer to place his right first finger on top of the hand-

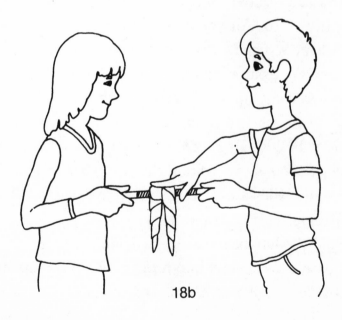

18b

kerchief, as in figure 18b. The finger must extend to cover both flaps of the rolled handkerchief. Wind the flaps around both finger and wand, *reversing* the direction of both ends. Follow the arrows in the illustrations exactly, making certain you do not cross the ends of the handkerchief while you are wrapping. When the winding is finished, tie the ends of the handkerchief in a small square or granny knot. The knot must conceal as much of the wrapping around the volunteer's finger as possible and will also help to hold the wrappings together.

Keep your right hand on the knot, and stand behind

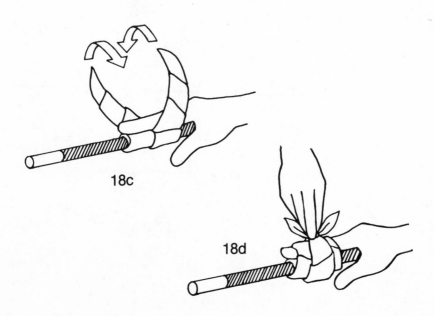

18c

18d

the wand so the audience has a clear view. With the thumb and fingers of your left hand, hold both sides of the handkerchief from below. Ask the volunteer to carefully remove the finger. At this point, you can say, "Hold the end of the wand very tightly because I am going to pull hard. This is a magic wand so I can pull the handkerchief right through . . . like *this*!"

Pull quickly upward on the knot, and the whole handkerchief will be free of the wand. Your left hand will keep the lower part of the handkerchief in place until the last moment. To the audience, the handkerchief will look as if it has passed upward through the middle of the solid wand. Hand the handkerchief to the volunteer, and say, "Thank you for your help. Would you please untie the knot? The wand still seems to have its magic powers."

✳ CARD MIND READING

For this mental magic the magician deals out twenty-one cards in three vertical rows of seven cards each. All cards are faceup. He or she asks a volunteer to choose a card but not to say which one. The magician asks the volunteer only which row the card is in. The magician gathers and deals the cards two more times, each time asking only which row the card is in. Then,

69

looking at the backs of the cards, the magician senses the correct card and turns it faceup.

The trick appears to involve mind reading but is really a mathematical game that works itself. Here are the steps. Hold an ordinary deck of cards so the backs are up. Moving from left to right, deal from the top of the deck three cards across faceup. Again from left to right, continue to deal until you have a total of

19a

seven cards in each vertical row, with each card partly overlapping the one above. There will now be three vertical rows with seven overlapping cards in each, all faceup.

Ask a volunteer to choose a card and to point out which row it is in. Suppose it is in the row on the right. Keeping the cards *faceup*, close each row without changing the order of the cards. The volunteer's row

70

is stacked faceup in between the other two rows. The stacked cards are then turned *facedown*. Again deal the cards faceup, left to right to make three vertical rows of seven cards each. Once again ask the volunteer to point out the row that contains the chosen card. Again gather the rows faceup, stacking the selected row in the middle. All steps are repeated for a third time. Once again the volunteer points out the row containing the chosen card, and once again you gather this row in between the other two.

Now turn the packet of cards *facedown*. If the steps have been followed properly, the selected card will be the middle card of the middle row. Thus, it will be exactly eleven cards down in the packet. Deal down to the eleventh card, and turn it over. Much to the surprise of the audience, it will be the card the volunteer picked out.

If the trick is presented as a mind-reading stunt, the audience will pay little attention to the mechanical steps. The magician can tell a story like this one: "This is a mind-reading trick, so I need a volunteer with a good imagination. As I deal out these cards, I would like you to choose a card from one of these three rows. Do not tell me which card you have chosen. Just create a picture of it in your mind. Now, without giving away

19b

the card, would you point out which row it is in?
Thank you. Let me deal the cards once again as you
continue to concentrate. Again, do not mention the
card, but simply point out which row it is in now. As
I make the final deal, please continue to think of your
chosen card. Which row is it in now?

"To help me tune into your card I use vibrations.
As I rub the back of each card I can feel the vibrations.
Your special card will have extra vibrations coming
from your mind . . . Yes, I believe this is your card.
Have I tuned in correctly?"

✳ RESTORED RIBBON

One popular magic trick is the cut-and-restored rope. With a ribbon you can do a simple variation that looks just as impressive. You need only some ribbon, a paper tube, and a pair of scissors. Get a brightly colored ribbon about a foot and a half long and about half an inch wide. The kind used for gift wrapping will be perfect. Figure 20a shows the pattern for the paper tube. Trace the pattern on tracing paper, and retrace the pattern onto ordinary white paper with carbon paper. Cut around the edges of the rectangular shape.

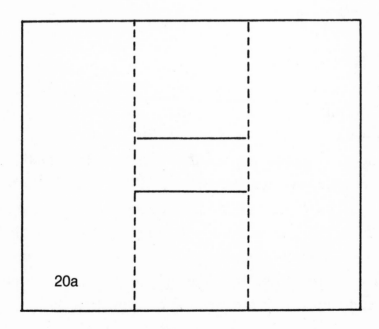

20a

Next cut slits along the two short lines in the middle of the pattern. Fold the flaps down on the dotted lines, and glue them together. You now have a narrow tube with two slits across the back.

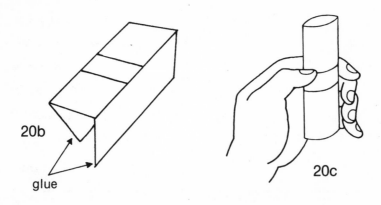

20b

glue

20c

Here are the moves and the story for the trick. First hold up the ribbon as you say, "Many magicians perform this trick with heavy rope, but I am going to do it with gift-wrapping ribbon." Set the ribbon down, and pick up the paper tube as if it were something very ordinary. Hold the tube upright in your left hand, with the two slits out of sight at the back. Place your left thumb between the slits and press lightly so that this part of the tube bends inward, leaving an open space at the back. Raise the ribbon again in your right hand and wave it around to focus attention on it.

Holding the ribbon by one end you can say, "Let's see what kind of magic can be done with this short piece of ribbon." As you speak, let the lower end of the ribbon drop down through the tube until half of the ribbon hangs out the bottom. The audience can see only the top and bottom of the ribbon, but you can see it passing through the open space between the slits at the back of the tube.

Now let the tube spring back into shape. Hold your left thumb over the part of the ribbon that shows between the slits. At this point, you can even swing your hand to the left for a moment casually to show the back of the tube. As long as your hand is in motion, no one will notice the slits in the tube.

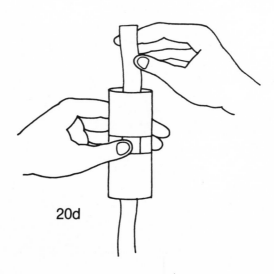

20d

Holding the tube in front of you again, take time to pull the ribbon up and down through the tube a little. The audience will be convinced that everything is still as it should be. Now pick up the scissors and say, "I hate to cut this beautiful ribbon, but I'm afraid that's what I have to do." Turn the tube sideways, tilted a little toward the audience with the ribbon hidden underneath. Insert one point of the scissors at the back between the ribbon and the tube. You can now neatly cut through the tube without harming the ribbon. The audience assumes that you have cut through both the tube and the ribbon inside.

Next slide your left thumb over the cut that the audience sees in the tube, temporarily holding the

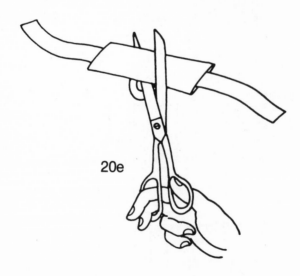

20e

halves of the tube in place. Swing the tube out to your left, holding it straight up and down. Reach over with your right hand, and slowly pull the ribbon up out of the tube. Smile at your audience and say, "I forgot to mention that this piece of ribbon was also magic." One by one let the two halves of the tube fall to the floor, where they will lie unnoticed. Face the audience as you hold up the completely restored ribbon, and move on to your next entertaining routine.

★ LOONY LOOPS

To do this trick, you need three strips of paper that have been made into three loops. The first strip has been made into a simple loop, and the other two loops contain twists. When these paper loops are cut in half lengthwise, the results are truly amazing.

To prepare the loops, first cut strips of newspaper one inch wide. Glue several strips together end-to-end to make three longer strips, each about four feet in length. Now cut a slit three inches long in one end of each long strip as shown in figure 21a. Form the first strip into an ordinary loop, and glue the ends together with white glue, such as Elmer's, or rubber cement. Be careful not to cover all of the slit. Loop the second strip in the same way, and then turn one end over to give it a half twist. Glue the ends in this position. Follow the same procedure to make a third loop, but give one end two half twists before gluing it in place.

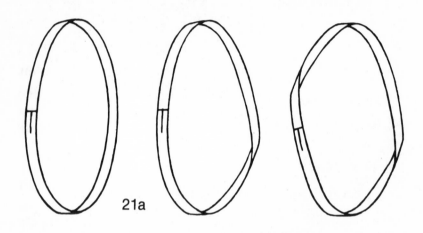

21a

Now you are ready for the story and the act. First pick up the loop with no twist. Insert the point of your scissors into the slit and continue the cut lengthwise. As you do so you can begin your story. "Not long ago I was in the Far East, where magicians are known for paper-cutting tricks. There I watched a famous magician do a routine with paper loops. First he cut a loop of paper in half down the middle to show that it would become two separate loops."

As you finish cutting all the way around, the single loop will fall apart into two narrow loops of the same size. Hold them up for the audience to see clearly. Let them drop and pick up the loop with *two* half twists as you continue your narration. "Then the magician sprinkled a little magic dust on another loop and said that it would give the loop extraordinary powers." Put one hand in your pocket and pretend to bring out a pinch of invisible powder that you sprinkle on the loop.

Now, with scissors, cut the loop lengthwise, as you did the first one. When you have cut all the way around the loop, the two sections will be mysteriously linked in a chain. Raise the top loop to show the lower loop linked permanently inside it.

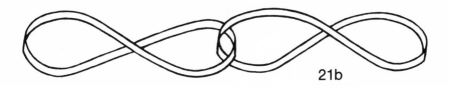

21b

Finally pick up the loop with only *one* half twist as you relate the rest of the story. "I was so amazed to see the linked loops that as soon as I returned home, I tried the trick for myself. I made a paper loop and sprinkled it with magic powder just as the famous magician had done." Pick up the loop, and begin cutting it lengthwise. At the same time, say, "I sliced it down the middle just the same way, but all I got was . . . *one long loop!*" Time your moves so that you finish the cutting just as you finish the story. To everyone's surprise, you now hold up one enormous complete loop, twice the diameter of the loop you started with!

21c

The trick works automatically if you have done the twisting and gluing correctly. The loop with one half twist is a special mathematical shape called a "Möbius loop," after the man who invented it. It seems to have only one edge so it cannot really be sliced in half at all but winds up as one double-sized loop. As for the loop with two half twists, it has been rotated completely around itself so that its two edges are automatically interlocked in advance. Use the mirror to practice the steps until they are perfect and will exactly match the story you have memorized. Act as excited as if you had really taken a trip to the mysterious lands of the East.

✷ FANTASTIC FLEXAGON

Although it looks different, this trick is based on the same principle as the Loony Loop with a half twist. This time the Möbius loop is flattened into a six-sided shape. There is a pattern on the front and another pattern on the back. But there is also a hidden pattern inside. When the figure is folded, or flexed, in a special way, the hidden surface comes into view and one of the other surfaces disappears. At the same time, each pattern turns inside out.

The pattern is on page 82. Place a piece of onion-skin or tracing paper over the pattern, keeping the paper firmly in place. Trace all lines with pencil and a ruler. Be sure to duplicate the dotted lines and the words *up*, *down*, and *glue*. Next you need a sheet of

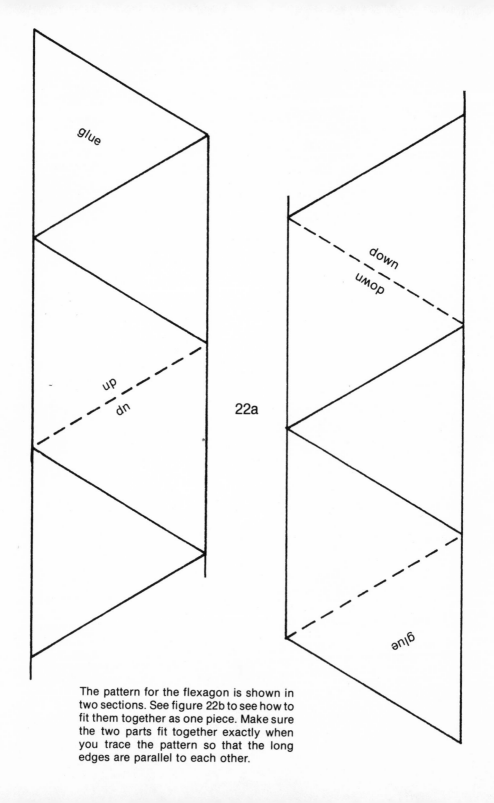

glue

up
dn

down
down

glue

22a

The pattern for the flexagon is shown in two sections. See figure 22b to see how to fit them together as one piece. Make sure the two parts fit together exactly when you trace the pattern so that the long edges are parallel to each other.

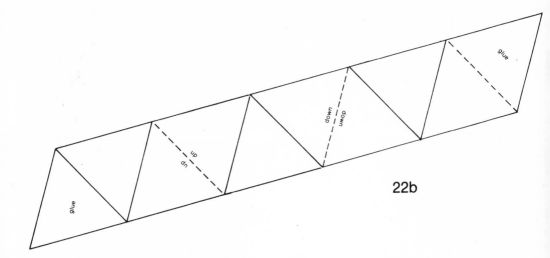

22b

extra-heavy white paper, such as construction paper. Place a sheet of carbon paper between the tracing and the construction paper, and tape the tracing paper into place. With sharp pencil and ruler, retrace all lines and markings of the pattern. Finally, on the construction paper, draw over the carbon lines with a fine-line pen so the pattern is clear and will not smear. Be careful to trace all lines exactly at each step.

With scissors, cut along the outer lines of the pattern. Fold the pattern up toward you at the dotted line marked *up*. Fold down away from you on the dotted line marked *down*. Use the back of a fingernail to crease each fold. Turn the pattern over so it looks like figure 22c. Bring the hidden flap marked *glue* to the front. Fold the top triangular piece down over the

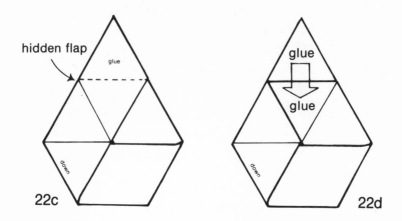

22c

22d

piece below so that the top triangles marked *glue* now touch. Fasten these flaps together tightly with white glue or rubber cement. Make certain the triangles overlap exactly.

With a fine-line pen and ruler, fill in the missing lines on both sides so that all opposite points of the figure are connected. The figure is now ready for folding. First fold the figure in half to bring matching corners exactly together. Reverse the fold on the same line, again matching the same set of corners. Crease with the back of a fingernail. Repeat the double folding steps with the two remaining long lines. Only the three long lines that connect opposite corners will be creased. The figure should now easily fold back and forth along any of the inside lines.

With thick felt markers, color one side of the hexagon yellow. Color the other side light orange. As soon as the colors are dry, you are ready to flex the figure. Hold as in figure 22e so that three points come together at the bottom. As soon as the correct points meet completely, the upper points can be opened out like a flower. The hidden white surface will come into view, and one of the colored surfaces will disappear! Bring the points together at the bottom again. Flexing the figure again will cause two more surfaces to change places. If the upper points do not open out, change the folds to bring the alternate set of three points together at the bottom. Only one set of points will work correctly.

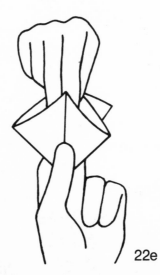

22e

The figure will open only if all three points meet completely below. As it is flexed for the first few times, flatten the figure and recrease all outer folds. Once the figure becomes limber it will flex easily, and the folds automatically fall into place.

The next step is to add designs to each of the three surfaces of the figure. Use a fine-line pen and a ruler. Fill in the shapes with felt markers. You can follow the designs suggested on these pages or you can invent your own. As you flex the figure, the shapes in the

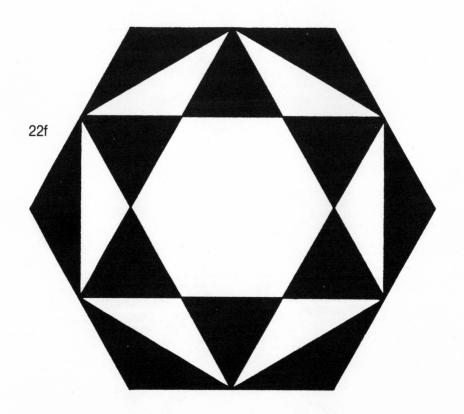

22f

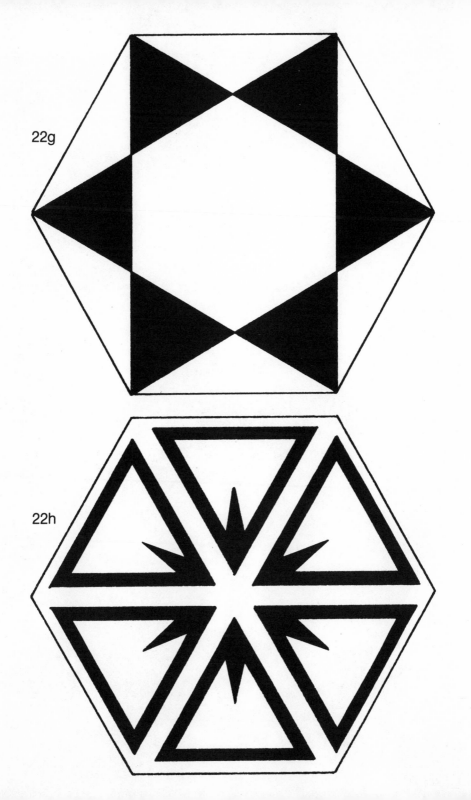

22g

22h

center of each surface will shift to the outer edges, or vice versa. This way there are three different surfaces, and each can be turned inside out. This amazing two-sided figure actually has six different surface patterns!

Because there is a hidden third surface and the basic shape is six-sided, this unusual figure is called a "tri-hexaflexagon," meaning a "three-six-bender." The flex-agon works itself. Once you learn how to flex it, its mysterious magic is at your command.

✳ TRAVELING PENNY

The last routine takes some practice but is basically easy to perform. To the audience, the magician seems to be holding up an empty matchbox. First he pulls out the drawer to show that the box is really empty. Next he closes the matchbox and sets it on the table. Then he takes a penny from his pocket and holds it up for everyone to see.

Now the magician begins to rub the penny into his elbow. In a moment, the penny vanishes and he shows that both of his hands are empty. He then calls for a volunteer from the audience. The volunteer opens the empty matchbox, and to the astonishment of the on-lookers the missing penny is found inside.

These steps are the ones the audience sees and remembers, but here is how the trick is actually done. First you need a small box of matches and two pennies that look almost exactly alike. Remove the matches from the box and store them in a glass jar or some other safe place. Slide the drawer most of the way out of the matchbox. You can now wedge a penny between the back edge of the drawer and the top of the box. It will be just out of sight and pinched tightly into place. Anyone who looks into the matchbox will assume it is empty.

To open your routine, you might say, "Here is a little matchbox I will be using later on." Without saying that the box is empty, simply turn it slowly so that

23a

23b

the empty drawer faces the audience. If you are careful, you can even hold the box upside down without
dislodging the penny. These actions will convince
everyone the box is empty more than if you actually
say so. Casually set the box down on the table again.
Then close it up with one hand at each end, causing
the penny to fall down inside the drawer unnoticed.

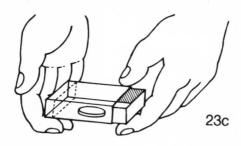

23c

Say to the audience, "Let me leave the box right here
where you can keep an eye on it."

Take the matching penny from your pocket and
hold it with your fingertips so it can be seen clearly
as you continue your story. "This is actually an en-
chanted penny. You will be amazed when I show you
what it can do. First I must place it on my elbow and
rub it to bring forth the magical spirits." Bend your
left arm as shown in figure 23d. Start rubbing the penny
into the back of your forearm as you say, "If I rub

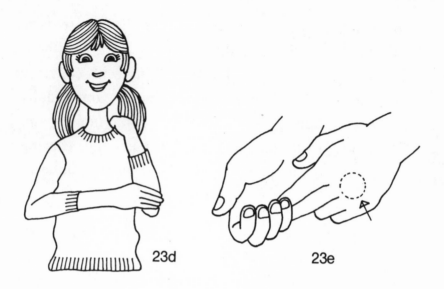

23d

23e

long enough the spirits will take control of the en-
chanted penny."

As you speak, look straight at your audience and not
at the penny. This part is *very important* because you
are going to pretend to drop the penny accidentally.
As you speak toward the audience, continue the rubbing motion with your right hand but let the penny
slip so it falls to the floor. Act as if it is nothing important. Just lean over slowly to pick it up again. Extend both arms toward the penny. Pick it up with your
left hand and pretend to transfer it to your right hand
as you stand up, but actually *keep the penny in your
left hand.*

Hold your left arm bent just as you did before, and pretend to go on rubbing the penny into your elbow with your empty right hand. Continue talking, explaining to the audience that sometimes quite a bit of rubbing is needed to bring on the magic spell.

You now have the penny in your left hand, which is at the back of your neck. You can easily drop the penny down inside your shirt, and no one will see what you are doing. Now you can pretend that the penny has been rubbed completely into your elbow. Brush your hands together and open them slowly toward the audience to show that both are empty. The mechanics of the trick are already over. But for the audience the best part is still to come.

23f

Step back a few feet from the table, and call on a volunteer to come forward as you say, "Would you please check the empty matchbox I put on the table at the beginning of the trick? . . . Oh, is there something inside? Yes, *there is the missing penny.* Would you hold it up so everyone can see it? Thank you very much for your help. It seems the spirits have been at work after all!" Shake hands with the volunteer, and bow deeply to the audience. You have shown them you are a real magician.

If you are careful and patient, those who watch your magic will have as much enjoyment as you have in accomplishing the tricks. Remember the helpful hints—have your materials ready, memorize the story and motions, use a mirror, test the trick out on a friend beforehand, and practice being a good speaker and actor. Choose the tricks you like best, and group them to suit yourself. Your magic will improve with practice so that even the simplest trick can look like a miracle. Believe in yourself, and you can have the satisfaction of becoming a really fine magician.

Index

95